NUCLEAR POWER
OF THE FUTURE
NEW WAYS OF TURNING
ATOMS INTO ENERGY

JOHN GIACOBELLO

THE ROSEN PUBLISHING GROUP, INC.
NEW YORK

Published in 2003 by The Rosen Publishing Group, Inc.
29 East 21st Street, New York, NY 10010

Library of Congress Cataloging-in-Publication Data

Giacobello, John.
Nuclear power of the future: new ways of turning atoms into energy /
by John Giacobello.— 1st ed.
p. cm. — (The library of future energy)
Includes bibliographical references and index.
ISBN 0-8239-3661-9 (library binding)
1. Nuclear power plants—Juvenile literature. 2. Power resources—Juvenile
literature. [1. Nuclear power plants. 2. Nuclear energy. 3. Power resources.]
I. Title. II. Series.
TK1078 .G52 2002
333.792'4—dc21

2001007930

Manufactured in the United States of America

CONTENTS

INTRODUCTION

When you hear the term "nuclear power," what do you think of? Is it Homer Simpson, half-asleep at the control panel of his town's nuclear reactor? Is it a super-market tabloid photo showing a baby born with three heads because its mother lived next to a nuclear power plant? Or maybe you've seen a horror movie in which the world is destroyed by nuclear weapons.

Of all the world's energy sources, people seem to have the greatest fear of nuclear power. Some of this fear is fueled by the history of nuclear power. Nuclear weapons were used at the end of World War II when the United States bombed the Japanese cities of Hiroshima and

A scene from *The Toxic Avenger, Part II*, a movie about a ninety-pound weakling who is transformed into a superhero by exposure to nuclear waste. Fictitious accounts of nuclear disasters in movies and on television create public fear of and misinformation about nuclear power.

Nagasaki. Pennsylvania's Three Mile Island nuclear power station had an accident in 1977. And in 1986 the former Soviet Union's Chernobyl nuclear reactor exploded in the Ukraine. Fear is also created or heightened by television shows, movies, and false or exaggerated news reports. When dealing with mass media, it can become difficult to sort out facts from entertainment.

This book looks at the facts of nuclear power. What are the real dangers? Can we learn to harness this energy without risking people's lives? What have we learned from past mistakes?

Nuclear power is a tool, and it can be used for the benefit or destruction of humanity. Let's explore the positive and negative ways it has been used already, the incredible advances and discoveries being made today, and this abundant resource's potential for our future.

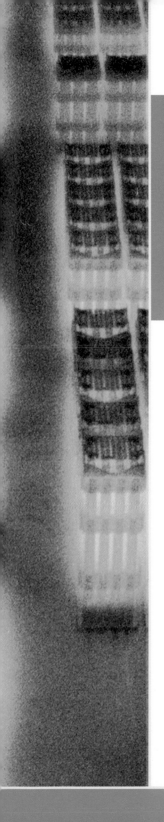

HOW NUCLEAR POWER WORKS

To end the war with Japan, an American plane dropped the first atomic bomb on Hiroshima, Japan, in 1945, causing devastation, pain, and suffering never before seen. But scientists knew that the power they had unleashed in wartime had many promising uses for peacetime. And so began the age of nuclear energy.

Uranium

Uranium, a radioactive chemical material, is the source of nuclear power. A dense metal found in Earth's crust, uranium was discovered in 1789. It was named after the planet Uranus. Scientists believe that uranium was formed around 6.6 billion years ago as a

Toxic clouds developed over Nagasaki, Japan, from the atom bomb that the United States dropped there in 1945.

result of huge explosions in space called supernovas.

Atoms are the tiny building blocks of all material on Earth. Atoms are made up of yet smaller particles: electrons, protons, and neutrons.

Protons and neutrons make up the nucleus, or center, of each atom. Electrons surround the nucleus. Nuclear energy is created when a uranium atom is split. For example, U-235 is an isotope of uranium. It contains 92 protons and 143 neutrons. If another neutron is added to the U-235 nucleus with enough force, the atom splits in two. When the atom splits, it releases energy in the form of heat. Often a few neutrons are also released in the split. These neutrons may split other nuclei, releasing more heat and more neutrons. This chain reaction is called nuclear fission. It is what makes nuclear power possible. The heat released by nuclear fission is what we use to produce electricity.

NUCLEAR REACTORS

The chain reaction of fission takes place in a nuclear reactor. Every reactor has a core that stores the uranium. Uranium pellets are put into fuel rods before the rods are inserted into the core. Fuel rods are about 3.5 meters (11.48 feet) long and a centimeter in diameter. Fission occurs when enough fuel rods are bundled

A power plant worker moves a hot and radioactive fuel rod to a water-filled pool, where it will be cooled and safely stored.

together in the core. The amount of uranium it takes to start the process is called the critical mass.

But critical mass alone cannot generate nuclear power. If the neutrons in the core move too quickly, the other uranium atoms cannot absorb them. This prevents fission from taking place. So the core uses a moderator to slow down the neutrons. Water, the most commonly used moderator, slows down the flying neutrons enough so they can be absorbed by other uranium atoms. The result is heat.

CONTROLLING FISSION

Nuclear chemical reactions are extremely powerful. Fission that is out of control can cause an explosion. To prevent an unwanted explosion, control rods are inserted into the core to absorb neutrons. Control rods are made of metal. Inside the core, the rods slow or stop the chain reactions by acting as "neutron sponges." Reactor technicians maintain the desired level of energy by inserting and removing control rods. This process is a lot like using the volume control on your stereo.

A worker at a Russian nuclear power plant prepares to start a nuclear reactor.

FROM FISSION TO ELECTRICITY

The next step in making electricity from nuclear power is to make steam. To do this, a coolant, usually water, travels through a pump into the core of the reactor. The process of fission heats the water. When the core is under high pressure, the water cannot boil away. The water absorbs the heat in the core. Then the water is pumped into a part of the reactor called the heat exchanger.

The core of a nuclear reactor is submerged in a water pool. The water functions to keep the reactor cool.

The heat exchanger takes the hot water from the core and uses it to heat other water. Why heat more water? Why not use the hot water just sent from the core? The problem with the coolant water is that, from being exposed to the fission process, it has become radioactive. The coolant water now gives off deadly waves that can kill animals and humans.

Small amounts of radioactivity are safe and even exist in nature. But highly radioactive substances are dangerous. They must not be allowed to leak radiation waves into the environment. To prevent people from being exposed to radioactive waves, the radioactive

Electric turbines at the Calder Hall Nuclear Power Plant in Cumberland, England. The turbines are driven by steam that has been generated by nuclear reactors.

coolant is run only through a carefully shielded area. In the heat exchanger, clean water is heated by radioactive water. The two types of water run through separate pipes that are very close together.

So now we have piping-hot, nonradioactive water that makes steam. The steam is the energy that is used to turn a turbine. There is a shaft inside the turbine that is wrapped in copper wire. The steam spins the shaft. The wires move past magnets installed in the turbine. As the wire moves through the magnetic fields, it becomes electrically charged. The electrical charge travels along the wire leading out of the turbine, to other wires that send it out to homes, offices, and factories as electricity.

TYPES OF REACTORS

The type of reactor just described is called a pressurized water reactor. In a boiling water reactor, no pressure is applied to the core to prevent the boiling of coolant water. This boiling water turns to steam. The steam is cooled and turned back to water at the end of the cycle.

Heavy water moderated reactors use "heavy water" as a coolant. Heavy water is made of two atoms of deuterium (a nonradioactive isotope of hydrogen) and one atom of oxygen. When heavy water is used, the uranium in the core does not need to be enriched, which makes it a cheaper form of fuel. The process of enrichment is described in the next section.

URANIUM AS A RESOURCE

There's lots of uranium in the earth, and we don't need much to generate power. We use much more oil and coal than uranium to create the same amount of electricity. But not all uranium is radioactive. Only about .7 percent of uranium is the isotope U-235, the isotope needed for fission. Most uranium is U-238. Because U-238 is not

This is U-235, the radioactive isotope of uranium that is used as fuel inside nuclear reactors.

fissionable, the uranium must first go through a process called enrichment to increase the concentration to U-235.

Enrichment is usually achieved through a process called gaseous diffusion. It sounds complicated, but gaseous diffusion is pretty simple. First, the uranium is converted to a gas called UF6. When this is done, it becomes possible to filter out much of the U-238 because it is heavier and more dense as a gas than U-235.

At an enrichment plant, the UF6 gas is forced through a filter with microscopic openings. The light U-235 moves easily through the filter, but the heavy U-238 has a hard time getting through. What comes out of the filter is UF6 gas, which has a higher concentration of U-235. The UF6 gas is converted back into a solid form. It's now a highly fissionable uranium powder, ready to be formed into pellets and inserted into fuel rods at a reactor.

But there is still plenty of U-238 in the uranium. When a U-238 atom absorbs a neutron, it does not fission. It becomes another element called plutonium. Plutonium is somewhat fissionable. About half of the plutonium fissions and provides one-third of a nuclear reactor's power. The rest of it is considered "spent fuel."

Spent fuel, which is highly radioactive, is stored in a facility where, over a very, very long time, the radioactivity decreases. There is still a small amount of useful material in the spent fuel that is separated for reprocessing. The rest is thrown away. Disposing of radioactive waste safely is one of the biggest challenges within the nuclear power industry.

Other Uses For Uranium

In addition to generating electricity at a power plant, uranium has many other uses. In medicine, X rays are used to see inside human bodies. Cancer is often treated using radiation therapy. And gamma rays are widely used to sterilize medical equipment.

Radiation is often used in farming to help preserve food and for pest control. It can also help strengthen growing crops. Industry uses radioisotopes to examine welds, to detect leaks, and to study the rate of wear of metals. They are also in some household items like clocks and smoke detectors. And radiation-equipped machines help police fight crime and aid the study of our environment.

2

NUCLEAR POWER YESTERDAY AND TODAY

The science of nuclear power is amazing. Its history is filled with brilliant people whose discoveries have changed the world. But these discoveries took place over a long period of time, and at high physical risk to the scientists.

THE NINETEENTH CENTURY: FIRST DISCOVERIES

In the early nineteenth century, John Dalton proposed the idea that everything is made up of tiny atoms. The atoms contain the substances we call elements. The work of John Dalton became the basis of atomic theory. Oxygen, copper, and

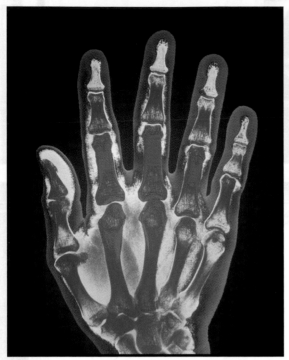

Creating X-ray images like this is one of the most common ways we use uranium.

calcium are just three of more than one hundred elements. Early atomic theory stated that atoms could not possibly be split.

In the 1890s, some scientists began to think differently about the atom. A German physicist named Wilhelm Roentgen was conducting an unrelated experiment. He accidentally discovered that unknown energy waves were strong enough to pass through solid objects. He had no idea what this energy was or where it came from. He called the waves X rays. These are the X ray waves doctors use today to see through layers of a patient's body.

Soon, other scientists began to explore X rays. Antoine Becquerel, a French physicist, thought the rays had something to do with sunlight. He tested his theory using uranium because it was the heaviest of the earth's natural elements. After exposing uranium to sunlight, Becquerel exposed the uranium to a plate of photographic film. Have you ever accidentally exposed a roll of film in your camera to the sun and ruined all the pictures? That's the same effect the uranium had on Becquerel's film.

Becquerel concluded that the uranium had absorbed the sunlight and released it as X rays to expose the film. But several days later, when it was cloudy, the uranium was still able to expose film. The uranium was producing its own energy! Becquerel was amazed. What did it mean? What allowed the uranium to continue creating energy waves, even after it was no longer receiving power from the sun?

This is where husband and wife scientists Marie and Pierre Curie stepped in. They tested radioactive uranium in search of answers. They discovered more radioactive elements: thorium, polonium, and radium. They concluded that radioactivity was an atomic property. Marie and Pierre Curie were the first people to understand that waves of energy came from atoms. They had discovered atomic energy!

Scientists knew that atoms were the smallest building blocks of elements. It seemed impossible that there could be anything smaller. But in 1897, Joseph John Thompson, a British physicist, did find something smaller than the atom. It was the negatively charged electron. Electrons surround the atom's core or nucleus.

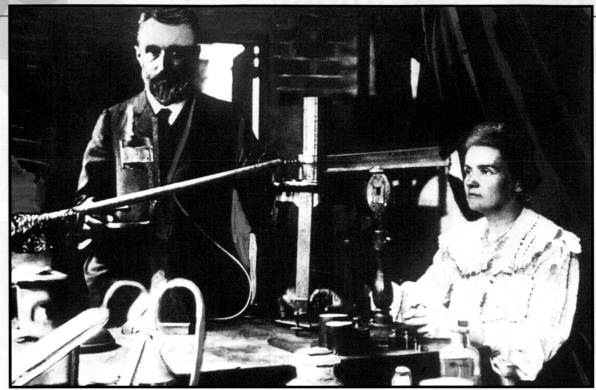
Pierre and Marie Curie are credited with having discovered atomic energy. They won the Nobel Prize in Physics in 1903 for their research.

Ernest Rutherford, Thompson's former assistant, studying the radiation given off by uranium, discovered what was happening in the nucleus. He saw that radiation was made up of positively charged alpha particles, as well as negatively charged beta particles.

THE EARLY TWENTIETH CENTURY: DEVELOPMENT AND DESTRUCTION

Rutherford experimented with alpha and beta particles. In 1919, as he shot alpha particles at the atoms inside the elements, he saw different kinds of reactions. When a nitrogen atom hit an alpha particle, the nitrogen atom emitted a positively charged particle. This particle became known as the proton. The nitrogen atom changed into an oxygen atom. Once scientists saw that they could change one element into another, they began to realize the potential power of the atom.

The next challenge for scientists was to harness the atom's power. For this, they had to learn how to make and control the right kind of reactions.

In 1932, British physicist James Chadwick discovered the neutron, a particle that carries no charge. Chadwick saw that because there was no charge, the neutron could enter the nucleus of the atom. When the neutron broke up part of the nucleus, the atom released a lot of energy.

Excited by this possibility, scientists began experiments in which they hit uranium with neutrons. In 1938, two Austrian physicists, Lise Meitner and Otto Frisch, explained in a paper that some uranium atoms were actually splitting in two, producing a neutron in the process.

Word about fission quickly spread. Scientists knew that a chain reaction of fission could produce a huge amount of energy for little cost. It would be cheaper to generate electricity with this new source of energy than with oil, coal, or water power. They also saw that if the atomic chain reactions were not strictly

Lise Meitner poses in a lab with Otto Hahn. Their research in radioactivity, both together and separately, led to the discovery of nuclear fission. When Hahn won the Nobel Prize in Chemistry in 1944, many in the science community thought that Meitner should have had a share in the prize.

controlled, they could set off the most powerful explosion in recorded history.

By 1942, American president Franklin D. Roosevelt created a project to build an atomic bomb. When these bombs were dropped on the Japanese cities of Hiroshima and Nagasaki in 1945, people around the world saw firsthand the terrible power of nuclear energy.

Experts hailed the beginning of a golden "atomic age," where cheap nuclear power would be available to all. In 1946, the American government created the Atomic Energy Commission (AEC) to start the atomic power business in America.

DID YOU KNOW?

The code name of the secret plan to develop an atomic bomb was the Manhattan District Project.

But the only atomic reactor to have been built so far had been used as a bomb. Could the same power that produced the deadly mushroom cloud also supply cheap electricity? In 1947, the AEC set up the Reactor Safeguards Committee to establish safety rules. By the early 1950s, the AEC built its first experimental reactors to demonstrate that atomic power could make safe electricity. In 1954, the first nuclear-powered submarine was built. By 1957, the first commercial nuclear reactor, in Shippingsport, Pennsylvania, began making electricity for public use.

THE ATOMIC SIXTIES AND SEVENTIES

By 1960, three commercial nuclear power plants were operating in the United States. Five years later, there were fifty. People raved that atomic power was the wave of the future. Environmental groups supported nuclear power because they were concerned about the pollution that was being caused by burning oil and coal. Nuclear power seemed too good to be true. In many ways, it was.

Scientists told the public that the small amount of radiation given off by a well-shielded nuclear reactor was perfectly safe, even

A 1999 aerial photograph of the Three Mile Island Nuclear Power Station in Pennsylvania.

for those living nearby. But many people were concerned about the risks of radiation. What if that well-shielded reactor was the scene of a terrible accident? What if radiation accidentally leaked?

Nobody really knew. The government did research, but hid most of the results from the public. In 1957, the AEC tried to determine what would happen in a nuclear accident. They kept that report top secret, too. In 1977, an organization called the Union of Concerned Scientists discovered a file listing past nuclear equipment failures and errors made by workers. Unfortunately, much worse problems were to come.

THREE MILE ISLAND

The first major nuclear power accident occurred at Three Mile Island, Pennsylvania. On March 28, 1979, a valve in the reactor's cooling system stopped working, blocking the flow of coolant to the core. A backup pump sent water to the area, which would have helped solve the problem. However, a valve connecting the pipes had been accidentally closed and the backup coolant was also blocked.

The emergency light flashing on the reactor's control panel to alert the workers was covered by a paper tag which prevented anyone from seeing it. The pressure and temperature at the core quickly climbed, creating the danger of an explosion.

A safety feature of the reactor caused a pressure relief valve to open and the intense pressure went down again. This valve remained open, and coolant that was left in the core began to boil. The escaping steam turned on the emergency cooling system. Unaware that the water was so low, plant operators turned off the emergency system. The remaining water boiled away, uncovering the hot core. A small explosion occurred, releasing radiation. Fortunately the amount of radiation that escaped was not considered dangerous.

Meanwhile, panic gripped the community. Confusing news traveled from nuclear officials to local authorities, then to the public. Public officials discussed evacuating the area, in case of a larger explosion. But operators gained control of the equipment, averting further problems.

This well-publicized accident did a great deal to damage the public's trust in nuclear power. It cost $1 billion to clean up the site, paid for by the company, its customers, and taxpayers.

An aerial view of the nuclear power plant in Chernobyl, Ukraine, a few days after an explosion occurred in the reactor on April 26, 1986.

CHERNOBYL

Chernobyl was once the site of a nuclear power plant in the Ukraine in the former Soviet Union. On April 26, 1986, Chernobyl became the site of the worst nuclear accident to date.

Chernobyl's operators were running safety experiments on the reactor's core. As they worked, they broke many of their own safety rules. Behind schedule, they were rushing to complete the experiments. They ignored warnings from their computer system telling them to shut down the reactor. The core had been damaged from too much heat, and control rods could not be inserted. Two large explosions sent deadly radioactive materials shooting into the environment.

Firefighters who rushed to the scene to put out the fire soon died of radiation exposure. Many of the pilots who flew overhead to drop boron, clay, lead, sand, and dolomite, to absorb the neutrons, died as well. Soviet authorities tried to keep the disaster secret. But as neighboring countries began to report excessive radiation levels in the air, the public was finally told. Only then were people who lived around Chernobyl evacuated, but they had already been exposed to deadly radiation.

Nuclear experts explained that Chernobyl was a poorly con-structed reactor and that the workers had ignored the safety regu-lations. Nuclear power plants in the United States were supposed to be much safer. At this point, there were over one hundred nuclear reactors in the United States, supplying 12.6 percent of the country's energy. Public opinion about nuclear power was reaching an all-time low.

THE UNCERTAIN NINETIES AND BEYOND

In 1990, construction was almost finished on a reactor in Midland, Michigan. At the last minute, the owners decided to make it a natural gas-burning facility instead. This was a sign of general feelings about nuclear power in the United States at the time.

Nuclear power was still growing in other parts of the world, however. By 1995, there were 424 nuclear reactors working worldwide. Fourteen reactors were being built in Asia. Thirty percent of Japan's electrical energy was nuclear.

In 1996, six U.S. nuclear power plants closed down. They claimed costs were too high and they couldn't make enough money. Canada closed a whopping twenty-one nuclear power plants because of safety problems. But nuclear power was still considered a possible future energy source. In the late 1990s, the Department of Energy released a study. That study showed U.S. energy consumption will most likely rise by 20 percent through 2020.

The government, feeling that nuclear reactors would have to be used to meet the extra demand, extended licenses for nuclear plants already built. The Nuclear Energy Research Initiative was created to fund the development of safer reactors. By 1999, public support was at 45 percent according to an Associated Press polling. This was down 10 percent from the same poll in 1989.

On September 30, 1999, there was an uncontrolled nuclear reaction at a plant in Takaimura, Japan. Several workers died. Meanwhile, many lawsuits for health damages in the Three Mile Island accident were reopened. Twenty years earlier, courts had dismissed them. Also, the University of Pittsburgh concluded a thirteen-year study which found cancer illnesses had not increased in the neighborhoods surrounding the plant. Small nuclear accidents in Buchanan, New York, and Los Alamos, New Mexico, have angered critics but caused no serious injuries.

As we have seen, safety is the most important issue when it comes to public approval of the nuclear power industry. The public wants to know if the job is being done safely. Safety will determine the future of nuclear-powered energy.

3 THE BUSINESS AND POLITICS OF NUCLEAR POWER

Atomic energy was under strict control of the U.S. government throughout the 1940s. First came the A-bomb and all of the military secrecy of it. Soon after, President Harry S. Truman created the Atomic Energy Commission (AEC) to look for safe and peaceful uses of this new technology. Private companies were not ready to put money into nuclear power which had only been used for war. So the AEC put together the Reactor Safeguards Committee and the Industrial Advisory Group. These agencies were meant to boost public confidence in nuclear power.

By the early 1950s, the government was showing their experimental reactors to possible investors. But utility companies were still not sure this strange new power source was safe. So in 1957, the government "sweetened the pot" for companies with the Price-Anderson Act. This law set a limit for how much a company would have to pay in the event of an accident. That year construction began on the first commercial power plant in the U.S. Many plants followed.

In 1964, the Private Ownership of Special Nuclear Materials Act became law, making it possible for utilities to purchase and own enriched uranium, which contains the isotope U-235 in a concentration above 20 percent. They could now use U-235 in their power plants. This was a big step in ending the monopoly the government had held over nuclear materials. It helped the private nuclear industry to expand.

The Nuclear Regulatory Commission

In 1974, the Energy Reorganization Act was passed. This split the AEC into two separate commissions. The Nuclear Regulatory Commission (NRC) would watch and make sure the nuclear power industry was safe. All companies running nuclear reactors had to report to the NRC. The Energy Research and Development Administration oversaw the nuclear weapons program.

The NRC was created to enable private companies to run nuclear power plants safely. A private utility company could build a nuclear power plant if they could pay for the NRC license. But only a reactor that met the NRC's standards would be granted a license to operate.

Qualified professionals from the NRC inspect all power plants regularly. They ensure that operators are not endangering themselves or the environment. They also establish guidelines to follow in preparing for emergencies. If there is an accident at a power plant, employees must follow procedures set by the NRC in dealing with the problem. Even natural disasters, such as earthquakes or floods, can create special dangers for nuclear reactors. The NRC has rules to follow in those situations as well. And the NRC even has regulations for how employees of the reactors are trained and supervised.

The NRC also oversees waste disposal. This is a controversial topic. Storing waste for up to fifty years allows radioactive isotopes in low-level waste to decay. Then it can be safely disposed. But highly radioactive wastes must be stored where they cannot do harm to any kind of life on our planet. The NRC oversees the safe transportation methods for these waste products. The NRC also regulates uranium enrichment facilities. As we saw in chapter 2, however, no method is foolproof.

LOW-LEVEL RADIOACTIVE WASTE POLICY ACT

All reactors produce both high-level and low-level radioactive wastes. Many people are willing to accept nuclear reactors in their

Nuclear waste management technicians sort and package low-level radioactive waste for shipment to a facility where it can be stored for ten to fifty years.

neighborhoods, but fewer are willing to accept a nuclear waste facility nearby. Everybody wants the energy, but nobody wants the waste.

The government was once again called in to solve this problem. Its solution for the low-level waste problem was the Low-Level Radioactive Waste Policy Act of 1980. Its goal was to spread out the burden of low-level waste disposal as evenly as possible across the United States. The states had to form compacts with states in the same region. The compacts had to work together to store the waste. One state in each compact would build a facility for the entire compact's disposal needs. That state would act as host for twenty years. Another state in the compact would then take a turn as host.

NUCLEAR WASTE POLICY ACT

Safe disposal of highly dangerous nuclear waste has been the biggest problem. In 1982, the Nuclear Waste Policy Act charged the Department of Energy (DOE) with finding geological sites where the waste could be buried so deep in the earth that no radiation could leak. This mission has been nearly impossible. Even today, no disposal technology has been perfected.

YUCCA MOUNTAIN

Since 1987, scientists have been studying the site of Yucca Mountain in Nevada to see if it would hold up as a place to store the highly radioactive material. Yucca Mountain has been their greatest hope because it is far from where people live. The closest city, Las Vegas, is 100 miles away.

Also, the area is extremely dry. There is little water beneath the ground because it hardly ever rains there. This is extremely important because water can become contaminated by radioactive material.

As of this writing, the secretary of energy has officially recommended Yucca Mountain to the president as the best repository site for highly radioactive materials based on careful consideration of the studies conducted so far.

ATOMIC ENERGY TODAY

Many agree that the American nuclear power industry has gone into a slump. The accidents at Three Mile Island and Chernobyl have turned most people off nuclear power. They say nuclear power's cheap, renewable resource is not worth the danger. In 1996, six United States nuclear plants closed. Each cited money problems. In fact, no new plants have been ordered since 1974. One power plant was built in Long Island, New York, but was shut down before it ever opened. The public is simply afraid of the dangers nuclear power presents.

Another problem has been a decrease in government funding since the 1970s. Keeping reactors running safely costs a lot of money. Power plants can experience equipment failure as they age. Replacing worn

Yucca Mountain, a proposed nuclear waste dump in Mercury, Nevada

parts, including possibly the core itself, makes older reactors more of a liability to utility companies than an asset. The dream of using cheap, powerful nuclear energy may be threatened.

Advocates of nuclear power are hoping to expand it in the next century. Earth's fossil fuel (oil, coal, and natural gas) resources are shrinking. Relying on oil coming from the Middle East is becoming less and less attractive to the United States. The DOE's Information Administration estimates that by 2020, U.S. energy consumption will have increased by 20 percent. To keep pace with that growth, we will need to build over 200 new nuclear power plants.

INTERNATIONAL NUCLEAR POWER

The future of nuclear power in the United States is uncertain. Nuclear power, however, is booming in some countries around the world. For example, almost 80 percent of France's electricity needs are met by nuclear power. Most of the French are comfortable with the reactors and have great confidence in their highly trained operators. While Germany's nuclear power accounts for 30 percent of its electric energy needs, Germany decided in June 2000 to phase out all of its nuclear plants. Other nations using mostly nuclear power include Belgium, Sweden, and Lithuania. All together, uranium supplies around 16 percent of the world's electricity. There are more than 430 reactors worldwide.

4 NUKES OR NO NUKES?

The issues and history surrounding nuclear power are complicated. If you're still not sure what to make of it all, you are not alone. Many people are still uncertain whether to support the use of nuclear power or not. An important step toward greater understanding of this future energy issue is to examine its pros and cons.

GLOBAL WARMING AND POLLUTION

One great hope for advocates of nuclear power today is the threat of global warming. When fossil fuels are burned, they give off carbon dioxide. This emission has been shown to trap heat in our atmosphere. Trapped heat raises the overall temperature

Clouds of carbon dioxide rise from a power plant powered by fossil fuels, polluting the environment.

of the planet. Global warming harms our farmlands, forests, and coasts, threatening our survival.

Nuclear fission provides energy without giving off damaging carbon dioxide. It has been estimated that using nuclear power today keeps as much carbon dioxide out of the atmosphere as taking ninety-four million cars off the road.

Besides carbon dioxide, fossil fuels also emit sulfur dioxide, toxic metals, arsenic, cadmium, and mercury, organic substances that can cause cancer. These pollutants cause damage to our health and environment. Properly maintained nuclear reactors give off small amounts of emissions. Some say the small increase in radiation they emit is harmful. These claims have yet to be proven. The nuclear industry is the only energy industry that is fully responsible for disposing of its own wastes.

The other side of this debate is the high costs of nuclear energy. Can enough reactors be built to make any real difference in the atmosphere's future carbon dioxide levels? Probably, but the costs would be high. It would mean replacing coal-fired power plants with nuclear power plants, costing trillions of dollars. It would also take decades to achieve.

ABUNDANCE

While our fossil fuels will eventually run out, uranium is one of our most abundant energy sources. We need a lot less uranium than fossil fuel to generate the same amount of electricity. We can reprocess uranium and use it again, so there will be less waste. The uranium in old nuclear weapons can be used to generate power. These are important ideas to consider when thinking about our future.

COSTS

The cost of nuclear power was once cheap. Today, however, the cost of generating nuclear power has increased tremendously. There is no longer government money to help power companies. The added expense of installing new safety equipment and storing nuclear wastes has made nuclear power much more costly. The statistics on this issue can be tricky. For example, the average production cost for generating nuclear power is 1.92 cents per kilowatt-hour. This is compared to 1.88 cents for coal-fired electricity, 2.68 cents for natural gas, and 3.77 cents for oil. The kilowatt-hour average, however, does not include the rising cost of updating reactors, maintaining them, or of storing waste.

A 1986 study of seventy-five U.S. reactors compared their original estimated construction costs with their final costs. The study found that the original estimates for constructing seventy-five reactors had been $45 billion. The final costs totaled $145 billion! *Forbes* magazine called the U.S. nuclear power program's economic handling "the largest managerial disaster in business history." Still, some people say that new and more efficient designs of reactors would work more efficiently and be safer to run. The total costs would then be much less.

Terrorism Risks

International terrorism is a great threat to nuclear power. Terrorists are trying to steal nuclear materials that can be used to make nuclear bombs. Many experts say that few terrorists have the knowledge or the ability to use such materials to build a bomb. But even planting the most common explosives in a reactor could result in a massive nuclear catastrophe, spreading deadly radioactive materials over a wide area. This would kill and injure hundreds or thousands of people without an atomic bomb ever actually having to be built. The Nuclear Regulatory Commission does not require that power plants be able to defend against these attacks in order to be licensed. Critics of nuclear power say this lack of security makes us all vulnerable to attack.

DID YOU KNOW?

In 1999, an Associated Press poll found that the American public's support for nuclear power had dropped from 55 percent to 45 percent.

HUMAN ERROR

The NRC makes sure nuclear power plants are as safe as possible. Yet human error is always possible. In fact, all nuclear accidents to date have been caused by human error. There is no way, then, to completely prevent accidents. Yet precautions can be made so that accidents cause minimal damage, as in the Three Mile Island accident. The Chernobyl accident, however, was disastrous on a grand scale. Experts point out that the Chernobyl reactor was poorly maintained with a highly unskilled staff. Such a reactor and staff would never meet the high standards of the United States's NRC.

Safety is one of the great stumbling blocks in the growth of nuclear power. Do we risk a potentially fatal nuclear accident, or do we risk destruction by pollution from fossil fuels and global warming? Weighing the consequences of each choice is an important part of our decision-making process. There are, unfortunately, no simple answers.

RADIATION

The question of danger from radiation given off by nuclear power plants lives on. Many experts have said that a reactor gives off no

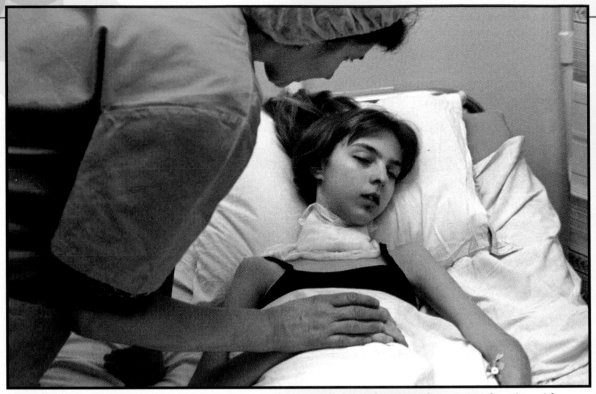

Radiation is thought to cause birth defects and increased rates of cancer. The young Ukranian girl in this photo suffers from thyroid cancer, believed to be a result of the Chernobyl explosion in 1986.

more radiation than already exists in nature and, therefore, poses no risk to any life on this planet. Others insist that any amount of radiation is dangerous to anyone who is exposed to it. There is evidence that exposure to enough radiation can lead to cancer and genetic mutations in offspring.

But the question of exactly how much is enough has yet to be answered. Some studies of cancer cases in relation to nuclear power plants have shown a higher number of cancerous diseases in those living near reactors. Yet other studies, including one performed on those living in the vicinity of Three Mile Island, have shown no relationship.

WASTE DISPOSAL

Opponents of nuclear power often point to the difficulty in disposing of highly radioactive substances. Supporters say that we can simply bury the wastes deep under the ground and seal up the hole. Opponents stress that we have not yet found a suitable place for that hole. Furthermore, the dangerous by-products are building up in temporary facilities all over the country. How sure can we be that the storage facility we choose will not be broken open by an earthquake or contaminate the water supply in the area?

Yucca Mountain has been found to have at least thirty-three earthquake fault lines running through or near the site. There is also a volcano close to Yucca Mountain that has been estimated to have erupted within the last 20,000 years. Some scientists are concerned about the possibility of waste products leaking from their canisters. They say a chemical reaction with the rock they would come into contact with could result in a massive explosion. For these and other reasons, most citizens polled in the area are against the dump.

And what about the risk of an accident in transporting radioactive waste to a disposal site? What if a truck transporting these substances overturned near your home? It could cause the spread of dangerous chemicals throughout your neighborhood. These are the questions perplexing those on both sides of the nuclear waste debate. Firm answers may determine the future of nuclear power.

5 THE FUTURE OF NUCLEAR POWER

What lies in the future for this controversial energy source? Studies show that by 2020, there could be as many as 8.1 billion people living on Earth. More people will need more energy. And less fossil fuel will be available. Can the nuclear power industry make advances in technology by then? Will those advances make fission seem as attractive to the United States as it does to an "atom-happy" nation like France?

TOMORROW'S REACTORS

The nuclear power industry is working to build better reactors. Designers of the next generation of power plants work hard to improve safety, reliability, and economics. More efficient reactors will give operators more time for safety procedures. Better-built reactors will offer stronger protection against radiation leakage. To reduce the risk of equipment malfunction, scientists are hoping to utilize natural forces, like gravity, to activate safety functions.

Simplicity is also a key aspect of new designs. The goal is to make the reactors as easy to operate as possible to minimize risk of human error. Inspection, maintenance, and repair procedures are also being simplified. Each task will require less work, less time, and less money. New digital technology will be used to ensure proper shut-down of the reactor in case of problems. Reactors of the future should also have a longer life span than the forty to fifty years of today's power plants.

Seawater

Seawater contains huge amounts of uranium. We have not yet begun to tap this resource. Uranium is abundant in Earth's crust, but mining it all will leave us with none. New technologies must be discovered. This is why learning to recover the element from our vast seas would add to our resources.

Japan has been highly motivated to find ways to do this. They must now import all of the approximately 6,000 tons of uranium they use in their reactors. Studies have proved that an ocean current, called the Black Current, off Japan carries approximately 5.2 million tons of uranium a year. Mining uranium from the sea could meet Japan's needs.

Scientists have been experimenting with ways to carry out the recovery. One very effective method that has been discovered involves uranium-absorbent cloth. Equipment has been designed to immerse this chemically treated cloth in the ocean. The water's current does all the work. As seawater passes through the cloth, uranium is absorbed. The element is then separated from the cloth and purified. Soon it's ready for use in fuel rods.

Even if every nation used sea-absorption methods, the balance of uranium concentration in the ocean still would not change. There's almost an endless supply of seawater. Perfecting this method would make for an excellent case in favor of nuclear power as a future energy source.

FUSION REACTORS

So far, the process of nuclear fission has been the only way to create nuclear power. But scientists are exploring another process. Someday nuclear fusion could be the alternative to fission.

Fusion is actually the opposite of fission. Rather than splitting atoms, the act of fusion joins them together. When a certain level of intense heat is reached, the nuclei of atoms can combine. The process of fusion releases even more energy than fission. And it does not require the use of radioactive substances like uranium. This is how the sun generates heat. It combines millions of light nuclei to form heavier ones.

Sounds great, so why don't we use it? The problem lies in raising temperatures to over 1,000,000°C, the necessary level for fusion to occur. Not only is it difficult to heat a substance to such a level, but it becomes nearly impossible to contain the heated substance. Right now, the process takes too long to be used by industry.

Fusion experiments are being conducted in a Russian nuclear reactor, the Tokamek. Researchers at the Tokamek have been attempting to generate enough heat for fusion reactions using plasma. Plasma is a gas that can become incredibly hot when a strong electric current is run through it. As a heat source, plasma has the added advantage of an electromagnetic field that prevents the surrounding container from being destroyed as the temperature soars. At this point, the plasma tends to cool before the fusion reaction can take place.

Tokamek has had some success in creating fusion. Experiments have made the temperature inside the reactor three times as hot as the core of the sun. But nuclear fusion as an energy source is still in the experimental stage. Researchers have not yet reached a point where fusion reactors are ready for commercial use. Right now, it takes more energy to start the reaction than the fusion it produces. So science continues to search for ways to reduce the energy input while increasing the energy output. When scientists find a way to make it more productive, fusion could become a safer alternative to fission.

The Tokamak Fusion Test Reactor, with which scientists hoping to create nuclear fusion have met limited success.

THE FUTURE OF
WASTE DISPOSAL

High-level (highly radioactive) waste disposal is the biggest issue facing the nuclear power industry today. Most in the business agree that burying the waste products deep in the ground is the best solution. This is currently the only disposal method being considered by the Department of Energy. But are there other possibilities?

Some people favor the idea of shooting the waste products into outer space. They call it "extraterrestrial disposal." The appeal of this idea is that it would send the potentially harmful waste as far away from Earth as possible. It would be gone for good, and we would never have to deal with it again. But extraterrestrial disposal is thought of as highly impractical today. Research, development, and completion are just too expensive. Risks would also play a role in the decision. These include the danger of a rocket that's holding nuclear waste malfunctioning while still in our atmosphere. The idea of extraterrestrial disposal has not been completely discarded, however. Yet this method is not likely to be explored in the near future.

"Nuclear transmutation" may sound like something you would hear in a science fiction movie. The concept actually *is* futuristic. Scientists are researching the possibility of transmuting, or transforming, radioactive waste into nonradioactive elements. If they could discover chemical reactions that would eliminate or reduce radioactivity in substances, the problem of waste disposal would shrink. While some advances have been made in research, this method remains a long-range goal.

Another option is disposal beneath the ocean floor. "Subseabed disposal" has one advantage: The seawater would dilute any leakage that could possibly happen. Some experts say it would then be made harmless. This method would also lend itself well to international cooperative disposal activities. However, no one has determined how such a massive amount of material would actually be placed under the ocean's floor.

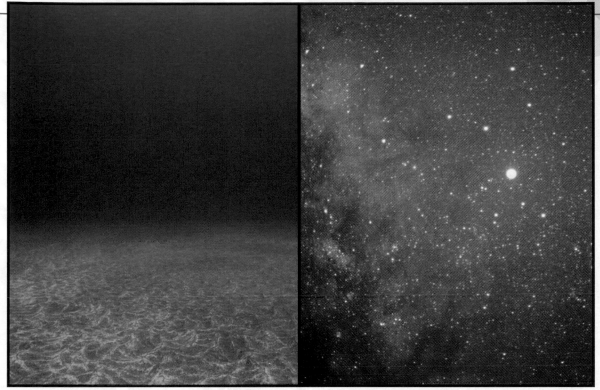
Some scientists advocate dumping nuclear waste beneath the ocean floor. Others want to send it into deep space.

OUR NUCLEAR FUTURE

Nuclear power has traveled a rocky road marked by both destruction and production. Public opinion still weighs heavily against it. But as the population continues to grow and our resources dwindle, we may have no choice but to face our fears. If we can put the past behind us, we will open up possibilities for the future. Or we may decide the risks are too great after all, and focus our attention on exploring other options. Let us hope that we can come to a decision before we reach a crisis situation. To quote an Indian physicist, the late Dr. Homi Bhabha, "No energy is more expensive than no energy."

GLOSSARY

alpha particle Positively charged particle that partly makes up radiation.

atom The tiny building blocks of all materials.

atomic theory The idea that everything is made of tiny atoms, which are made of substances called elements.

beta particle Negatively charged particle that partly makes up radiation.

control rods Rods made of metal, such as boron steel or cadmium, that absorb neutrons in a reactor's core.

core The center of a nuclear reactor, where uranium is placed to start a reaction.

critical mass The amount of uranium it takes to start the process of fission.

electrons Tiny particles that surround the nucleus of an atom.

element Any material that cannot be broken down into a more basic substance.

enrichment The chemical process that increases the concentration of isotope U-235 in uranium.

fuel rods Tubes into which uranium pellets are placed; the fuel rods are then put into a nuclear reactor's core.

gaseous diffusion The process of converting uranium to gas and separating the isotopes.

heat exchanger The area of a reactor that takes the hot water from the reactor's core and uses it to heat other water.

isotopes Different forms of the same element. The centers have the same protons but different numbers of neutrons.

moderator Water used to slow down the flying neutrons in a reactor's core so that they can be absorbed by other uranium atoms.

neutrons Particles packed into the nucleus of an atom, along with protons.

nucleus Center of an atom.

protons Particles packed into the nucleus of an atom, along with neutrons.

radioactive Material that, because of its exposure to fission, emits powerful waves that are harmful to humans.

spent fuel Uranium that is not fissionable; also called nuclear waste.

supernovas Massive explosions in space that are thought to have created uranium.

turbine Equipment in a power plant that generates electricity when turned by steam.

uranium Dense metal found in Earth's crust.

FOR MORE INFORMATION

Alliance for Nuclear Accountability
1801 18th Street NW, Suite 9-2
Washington, DC 20009
(202) 833-4668
Web site: http://www.ananuclear.org

Canadian Nuclear Society
480 University Avenue, Suite 200
Toronto, ON M5G 1V2
(416) 977-7620
Web site: http://www.cns-snc.ca

Laws and Regulations: USA States—Radiation Control
900 Ogden Avenue #337
Downers Grove, IL 60515
(630) 221-9116
Web site: http://www.rmis.com/db/lawradia.htm

Nuclear Regulatory Commission
(800) 368-5642
Web site: http://www.nrc.gov

U.S. Department of Energy
1000 Independence Avenue SW
Washington, DC 20585
(800) DIAL-DOE (342-5363)
Web site: http://www.energy.gov

Yucca Mountain Project
U.S. Environmental Protection Agency
1200 Pennsylvania Avenue NW (6608J)
Washington, DC 20460
(800) 331-9477
Web site: http://www.epa.gov/radiation/yucca

WEB SITES

Due to the changing nature of Internet links, the Rosen
Publishing Group, Inc., has developed an online list of Web
sites related to the subject of this book. This site is updated
regularly. Please use this link to access the list:

http://www.rosenlinks.com/lfe/nucl/

FOR FURTHER READING

Andryszewski, Tricia. *What to Do About Nuclear Waste.* Brookfield, CT: Millbrook Press, 1995.

Cheney, Glenn Alan. *Chernobyl: The Ongoing Story of the World's Deadliest Nuclear Disaster.* New York: Maxwell Macmillan International, 1993.

Daley, Michael J. *Nuclear Power: Promise or Peril.* Minneapolis, MN: Lerner Publications Co., 1997.

Galperin, Anne. *Nuclear Energy, Nuclear Waste.* New York: Chelsea House Publishers, 1992.

Henderson, Harry. *Nuclear Power.* Santa Barbara, CA: ABC-CLIO, Inc., 2000.

Hesse, Karen. *Phoenix Rising.* New York: Holt, 1994.

Lampton, Christopher. *Nuclear Accident.* Brookfield, CT: Millbrook Press, 1992.

Nordhaus, William D. *The Swedish Nuclear Dilemma: Energy and the Environment.* Washington, DC: Resources for the Future, 1997.

Paul, T.V. *Power Versus Prudence: Why Nations Forgo Nuclear Weapons.* Montreal: McGill-Queen's University Press, 2000.

BIBLIOGRAPHY

Jungk, Robert, and James Cleugh (translator). *Brighter Than a Thousand Suns: A Personal History of the Atomic Scientists*. New York: Harvest Books,1970.

Medvedev, Zhores A. *The Legacy of Chernobyl*. New York: W.W. Norton & Company, 1992.

Morris, Robert C. *The Environmental Case for Nuclear Power: Economic, Medical, and Political Considerations*. St.Paul, MN: Paragon House, 2000.

Scheider, Walter. *A Serious but not Ponderous Book about Nuclear Energy*. Ann Arbor, MI: Cavendish Press, 2001

Waltar, Alan E. *America the Powerless: Facing Our Nuclear Energy Dilemma*. Madison, WI: Medical Physics Pub Corp., 1996.

INDEX

CREDITS

ABOUT THE AUTHOR

John Giacobello is a freelance writer living in New York City.

PHOTO CREDITS

Cover © Premium Stock/Corbis; pp. 4–5, 40–41, 48–49 © Corbis Royalty Free; p. 6 © The Everett Collection; pp. 8–9, 55 (right) © Roger Ressmeyer/Corbis; pp. 10, 22, 32–33 © Bettmann/Corbis; p. 11 © Tim Wright/Corbis; pp. 12, 26, 28, 36, 38, 46, 53 © AP/Wide World Photos; p. 13 © Yann Arthus-Bertrand/Corbis; pp. 14, 18–19 © Charles E. Rotkin/Corbis; pp. 16, 24 © Photo Researchers, Inc.; p. 20 © Michael Freeman/Corbis; p. 42 © Robert Estall/Corbis; p. 55 (left) Ralph A. Clevenger/Corbis.

DESIGN AND LAYOUT

Thomas Forget